Ketogenic Dess

Delicious Ketogenic Dessert Recipes For Quick Weight Loss

Copyright ©

All rights reserved. No part of this book may be reproduced, stored in a retrieval system, or transmitted in any form or by any means, electronic, mechanical, photocopying, recording, scanning, or otherwise, without the prior written permission of the publisher.

Disclaimer

All the material contained in this book is provided for educational and informational purposes only. No responsibility can be taken for any results or outcomes resulting from the use of this material.

While every attempt has been made to provide information that is both accurate and effective, the author does not assume any responsibility for the accuracy or use/misuse of this information.

Table of Contents
Introduction

Ketogenic Chocolate Cheesecake

Ketogenic Peanut Butter Cups

Microwave Keto Chocolate Cake

Coconut Fudge Bites

Keto Brownies

Coffee Cheesecake

Creamy Fudge

Lava Cake

Cheesecake Mousse

Quick Ketogenic Cheesecake

Lemon Mousse

Cream Cheese Coconut Bites

Chocolate Fudge Cake

Mocha Pudding

Peanut Butter Balls

Ketogenic Carrot Cake

Keto Cheesecake Bites

New York Style Cheesecake

Ketogenic Lemon Cheesecake Bars

Peanut Butter Cheesecake

Berry Cheesecake Bites

Keto Chocolate Mousse

Ketogenic Coconut Cream Pie

Ketogenic Almond Cookies

Introduction

Ketogenic Chocolate Cheesecake

Ingredients

1 cup low-carb chocolate cookie crumbs

1/4 cup butter, melted

3 tablespoons Splenda Granular

1/2 cup finely chopped macadamia nuts, pecans, or almonds

3 eggs, separated

3 (8 ounce) packages cream cheese, at room temperature

1 cup sour cream

1 cup Splenda Granular

2 tablespoons low-carbohydrate baking flour substitute

6 ounces low-carbohydrate, dark chocolate, melted

3 ounces low-carbohydrate, dark chocolate, melted

3 tablespoons finely chopped macadamia nuts, pecans, or almonds

Directions

Combine cookie crumbs, butter, 3 tablespoons Splenda, and nuts. Press evenly in the bottom of a 9 inch springform pan.

Chill crust while preparing the filling. Preheat oven to 350 degrees F (175 degrees C)

In a large bowl, whip egg whites until stiff but not dry.

In another large bowl, beat cream cheese, sour cream, 1 cup Splenda, and flour substitute until smooth. Beat in egg yolks one at a time, blending well after each addition.

Gently fold whipped egg whites into cream cheese mixture. Spoon batter into prepared crust. Slowly swirl 6 ounces of melted chocolate through cheese mixture to give a marbled effect.

Place pan on a cookie sheet in the preheated oven, and bake 60 to 70 minutes or until set. Turn off oven, and allow cake to cool in the oven with the door open. When cool, transfer to the refrigerator, and chill overnight.

Spread 3 ounces of melted chocolate on a cookie sheet. Sprinkle with remaining chopped nuts, and then refrigerate until chilled. Scrape chocolate from pan to form slivers.

Decorate cake with chocolate slivers by heaping over the top, and pressing vertically onto the sides of the cake.

Ketogenic Peanut Butter Cups

Ingredients

½ cup unsalted butter

1 ounce unsweetened baking chocolate

⅓ cup Splenda granular

1 tablespoon half-and-half or 1 tablespoon cream

4 tablespoons peanut butter

¼ cup chopped walnuts (or other nuts)

Directions

Heat butter, chocolate, and Splenda on HIGH in the microwave until the mixture is melted, 60-90 seconds.

Stir the half & half or cream and the peanut butter into the melted mixture.

Line 10 muffin tins with cupcake papers. Place a sprinkle of nuts in bottoms of each tin.

Divide chocolate mixture evenly between the 10 tins. Freeze until firm.

Microwave Keto Chocolate Cake

Ingredients

1/4 cup almond flour

1 tablespoon cocoa

1/4 teaspoon baking powder

3 tablespoons plus 1 teaspoon granulated Splenda or equivalent liquid Splenda

2 tablespoons butter, melted

1 tablespoon water

1 egg

Directions

Mix the almond flour, cocoa, baking powder and granulated Splenda, if using, in a 2-cup glass measuring cup.

Stir in the liquid Splenda, if using, butter, water and egg. Mix well with a spoon or fork.

Scrape batter down evenly with a rubber spatula. Cover with plastic wrap and vent by cutting a small slit in center.

Microwave on HIGH 1 minute until set but still a little moist on top

Cool slightly and serve warm topped with whipped cream or cool completely and frost as desired.

Coconut Fudge Bites

Ingredients

1 ½ cups walnuts

½ cup flaked unsweetened coconut, toasted

¼ cup extra-dark cocoa powder

¼ cup coconut oil

½ teaspoon coconut extract

12 (3 1/2 g) packages artificial sweetener

¼ cup flaked unsweetened coconut, toasted

1 (3 1/2 g) packet artificial sweetener

1 pinch salt (optional)

Directions

Toast your coconut in a 350F degree oven, stirring often. Remove when your coconut is golden brown and cool.

Put walnuts in a food processor and process on low until they are pulverized and resemble coarse sand.

Add the next five ingredients and process until completely blended and the mixture clumps together.

Using a one inch scoop or two tablespoons, portion mixture onto a cookie sheet in 14 balls. Refrigerate until firm, about an hour.

If desired, roll ball in hands to make more symmetrical. Put remaining 1/4 cup coconut, packet of sweetner and tiny pinch of salt in ziplock bag, shaking to combine.

Put all 14 balls in the ziplock bag at once and shake to evenly distribute coconut coating.

Keto Brownies

Ingredients

6 tablespoons butter, softened

8 ounces cream cheese, softened

1 cup granular Splenda or equivalent liquid Splenda

2 eggs

4 ounces unsweetened chocolate, melted

3 ounces almond flour (3/4 cup)

1 teaspoon baking powder

1 teaspoon vanilla

Directions

Cream the butter and cream cheese in a large bowl. Add the Splenda and eggs; beat well.

Add the chocolate. Mix the almond flour and baking powder; add to the batter along with the vanilla.

Spread in a greased 8x8" baking pan.

Bake at 350° 20-25 minutes, until a toothpick comes out clean.

Coffee Cheesecake

Ingredients

1 packet unflavored gelatin

1/2 cup coffee, cold or room temperature

2 teaspoons instant coffee granules

2 cups heavy cream

16 ounces cream cheese, softened

1 cup granular Splenda or equivalent liquid Splenda, divided

1 teaspoon vanilla

Chocolate shavings, optional

Directions

In a medium bowl, whip the cream with 1/2 cup of the Splenda until stiff. Place the whipped cream in the refrigerator until needed. There's no need to clean the beaters. You can use them later for the cheese mixture.

In a small pot, sprinkle the gelatin over the cold coffee and let soften 5 minutes. Heat and stir over low heat to dissolve the gelatin completely.

Do not boil. You can also dissolve the gelatin in the microwave by heating it about 30 seconds or so on HIGH. Stir until completely dissolved. Stir in the instant coffee granules until dissolved.

Cool to room temperature. Add the remaining 1/2 cup Splenda and the vanilla to the cooled gelatin mixture.

Beat the cream cheese until creamy and smooth. Gradually beat the gelatin mixture into the cream cheese until well blended and slightly fluffy. Chill the batter until slightly thickened, about 20-30 minutes, stirring every 10 minutes to prevent lumps.

Very gently fold in the whipped cream a little at a time.

Spread in a greased 9-inch pie plate and chill until set, about 5-6 hours.

Creamy Fudge

Ingredients

¼ cup butter

2 ounces unsweetened chocolate (2 squares)

24 (1 g) packets Equal sugar substitute

1 teaspoon vanilla extract

8 ounces cream cheese, softened (not fat free)

½ cup chopped nuts (optional)

Directions

Melt butter over low heat.

Add chocolate and stir until melted. Remove from heat and stir in sweetener and vanilla.

Combine the chocolate mixture with the cream cheese and beat until smooth.

Stir in nuts and spread in lightly greased 8-inch square pan.

Refrigerate until firm.

Lava Cake

Ingredients

1 tablespoon butter

1/4 teaspoon vanilla

1 tablespoon heavy cream

1 egg

2 tablespoons cocoa

1 tablespoon powdered Truvia

Pinch salt

1 square 70% cacao chocolate

Directions

Put the butter in a 2-cup glass measuring cup; cover with plastic wrap.

Poke a couple small holes in the plastic with a toothpick. Microwave about 20 seconds to melt the butter.

Whisk in the vanilla, cream and egg until well blended. Add the cocoa, Truvia and salt; whisk until smooth.

Cover with plastic wrap and microwave on high about 30-40 seconds or just until it is slightly set.

Remove from the microwave and cut a small X in the top of the cake with a sharp paring knife.

Insert the chocolate pieces, one on top of the other, so that they don't show too much from the top.

Cover again and microwave another 30 seconds or so or until the cake is fully set.

Invert the cake onto a dessert plate and let it cool before serving.

Cheesecake Mousse

Ingredients

8 ounces cream cheese, softened

1 cup heavy cream

1 (1/3 ounce) box sugar-free jello (your choice of flavor)

½ cup boiling water

Directions

Melt sugar free jello in boiling water.

Stir well to dissolve and cool slightly.

Beat softened cream cheese until smooth and stir in cooled jello.

Lightly fold in heavy cream until well mixed.

Pour into serving dishes and put in fridge to chill at least 3 hours.

Ketogenic Cheesecake

Ingredients

2 Eggs

2 tsp vanilla extract

1 1/2 cups sour cream

1/2 cup Splenda granules (or other artificial sweetener)

16 oz cream cheese, softened.

2 tbsp melted butter.

Directions

In a large bowl, blend together eggs, vanilla, sour cream and splenda.

Slowly add butter and cream cheese.

Spoon about 1/2c mix into another bowl and add raspberry flavoring (sugar free). Mix well.

Spoon remaining mix into a 10 inch spring release pan or 12 ramekins.

Add dollops of raspberry batter on top and swirl thru.

If desired, you can make a crust from 1 1.2 cups ground almonds, 1/4 cup splenda and 1/4 butter.

Mix all together to form a crust and line pan or ramekins.

Bake in 350F oven for 20-25 min if cooking ramekins, 35-40 min for spring pan. When finished chill in fridge for firmer cake.

Garnish with fresh raspberries and whipped cream if desired.

Quick Ketogenic Cheesecake

Ingredients

3/4 cup heavy cream

2 teaspoons vanilla

2 eggs

1 cup granular Splenda or equivalent liquid Splenda

1/2 cup Carbquik

16 ounces cream cheese, cubed and softened

Directions

Preheat oven to 350F.

Put all of the ingredients except the cream cheese in a blender. Blend on high speed 15 seconds. Add the cream cheese; blend 2 minutes.

Pour into a well-greased 9-inch pie plate.

Bake at 350F° 35-40 minutes or until a knife inserted in the center comes out clean. Chill well before serving.

Lemon Mousse

Ingredients

½ cup butter

9 egg yolks

4 egg whites

4 lemons, juice of

2 teaspoons grated lemons, zest of

5 packets sugar substitute (of choice)

1 ½ cups heavy cream

1 teaspoon vanilla extract

Directions

Melt butter in a medium saucepan over low heat. Remove from heat and whisk in yolks one at a time.

Beat in lemon juice, zest and 4 packets sugar substitute.

Chill.

Beat egg whites and extract with 1 packet sugar substitute. Fold into the chilled egg yolk mixture.

Beat cream with vanilla extract and fold into the mixture. Fold into the chilled egg yolk mixture.

Spoon into 8 serving cups and chill for at least 2 hours

Cream Cheese Coconut Bites

Ingredients
8 ounces cream cheese, softened

1/2 cup unsalted butter, softened

4 eggs

1 cup granular Splenda or equivalent liquid Splenda

2 1/2 teaspoons vanilla

1 cup coconut flour, sifted

1/4 cup unsweetened coconut

Directions
Preheat oven to 350F.

Beat the cream cheese and butter with an electric mixer until light and fluffy. Add the eggs one at a time, beating well. Add the Splenda and vanilla; beat well. Add the coconut flour and beat well.

Spread the dough in an 11x7" baking pan that has been lined with foil and greased. I also put a sheet of parchment paper in the bottom. Sprinkle the coconut over the top and very lightly press it into the dough.

Bake at 350F° 20-25 minutes until the top is browned.

Cool completely on a rack then cut into 24 squares.

Chocolate Fudge Cake

Ingredients

2 tablespoons whey protein isolate

2 tablespoons almond flour

2 tablespoons cocoa

1/4 teaspoon baking powder

2 tablespoons butter, melted

3 tablespoons plus 2 teaspoons granulated Splenda or equivalent liquid Splenda

1/4 teaspoon vanilla

1 tablespoon water

1 egg

Frosting

1/4 cup heavy cream

1/4 teaspoon instant coffee powder, crushed

4 teaspoons granulated Splenda or equivalent liquid Splenda

1 tablespoon cocoa, sifted

Directions

Melt the butter in a 2-cup glass measuring cup. Stir in the Splenda, vanilla and water. Sift the wheat protein isolate, almond flour, cocoa and baking powder together; stir into the butter mixture.

Break the egg into the measuring cup and mix well with a fork.

Scrape down the batter with a small rubber spatula. Cover with plastic wrap and vent by cutting a small slit in center. Microwave on high 1 minute until nearly set, but still a little moist on the top.

Cook about 10 seconds or so more if too moist.

Invert onto a small plate; cool completely.

To Make Frosting:
Pour the cream into a small, deep mixing bowl. Add the instant coffee powder and stir until dissolved; add the Splenda.

With a wire whisk, whip the cream until it just starts to thicken.

Slowly blend in the cocoa and whish just a few seconds until thick.

Pour frosting evenly on cooled cake.

Mocha Pudding

Ingredients

1 (1 ounce) box sugar-free instant chocolate pudding mix

¾ cup cold water

1 tablespoon unsweetened cocoa powder

4 ounces cream cheese

½ pint heavy whipping cream

1 teaspoon peppermint extract or 1 teaspoon almond extract or 1 teaspoon coffee extract

Directions

Put all ingredients in a bowl.

Whip until combined.

Chill and serve.

Peanut Butter Balls

Ingredients

1/4 cup low carb nutlike cereal nuggets

2 tablespoons extra crunchy peanut butter

1 (0.75-ounce) package chocolate sugar-free dairy shake mix

1 packet sugar substitute

1 1/2 tablespoons water

1/2 teaspoon honey

1/2 teaspoon vanilla extract

Directions

Combine all ingredients in a medium bowl, stirring until moist and well blended.

Shape mixture into 8 (1-inch) balls.

Cover and chill.

Ketogenic Carrot Cake

Ingredients

1 cup unblanched almond flour

1 cup finely ground unsweetened coconut

1 teaspoon baking powder

1 teaspoon baking soda

1/4 teaspoon salt

1 1/2 teaspoons cinnamon

1/4 teaspoon ground ginger

1/8 teaspoon ground nutmeg

1/8 teaspoon xanthan gum

1 cup granular Splenda or equivalent liquid Splenda

1 1/2 teaspoons vanilla

1/2 teaspoon pineapple extract, optional

2 tablespoons oil

1 teaspoon blackstrap molasses

2 eggs

1/4 cup heavy cream

4 ounces carrot, finely grated

Frosting:

8 ounces cream cheese, softened

1/2 cup unsalted butter, softened

1/2 cup granular Splenda or equivalent liquid Splenda

1 teaspoon vanilla

Directions

Put everything except the frosting ingredients in a medium mixing bowl and beat well with an electric mixer until you have a very thick batter.

Spread in a greased 8 1/2 x 6 1/2" baking pan.

Bake at 350F for 25-30 minutes. The cake is done when the center is firm when pressed.

Cool completely before frosting.

Beat the frosting ingredients in a small mixing bowl with an electric mixer until fluffy. Spread over the cooled cake evenly.

Keto Cheesecake Bites

Ingredients

12 ounces cream cheese, softened

3 eggs

1/2 cup heavy cream

1/2-3/4 sugar free syrup, vanilla flavor

1 teaspoon vanilla

Directions

Beat the cream cheese until fluffy. Beat in the eggs, then the remaining ingredients until well blended.

Pour into a buttered 8x8" baking pan. Bake 350º 50-60 minutes until a knife inserted in the center comes out clean and the cheesecake is golden brown on top.

Cool completely before cutting; chill well before serving.

New York Style Cheesecake

Ingredients

Crust:
1/4 cup pecans, finely ground, 1 ounce

1/4 cup almonds, finely ground, 1 ounce

1/4 cup walnuts, finely ground, 1 ounce

3/4 cup almond meal, 3 ounces

2 tablespoons butter, melted

Filling:
24 ounces cream cheese, softened

1 1/3 cups granular Splenda or equivalent liquid Splenda

5 eggs, room temperature

1/4 cup whey protein isolate or wheat protein isolate

2 teaspoons vanilla

2 teaspoons lemon juice, you'll need 1 small lemon

16 ounces sour cream

Directions

Mix the nuts and almond meal with the melted butter; press onto the bottom and 1 1/2 inches up sides of a 9-inch springform pan. Set aside while mixing the filling.

Beat the cream cheese until light and fluffy, keeping the mixer on a low setting throughout the beating and mixing process. Add the granular Splenda a little at a time and continue beating until creamy.

Add one egg at a time and beat very briefly after each egg. When the eggs have been mixed into the cream cheese add the whey or wheat protein powder, vanilla and lemon juice, mix briefly, just until combined. Add the sour cream last and beat briefly.

Pour the cream cheese mixture into the springform pan. Bake at 325F° (300F° for dark, nonstick pan) for 1 hour and 15 minutes.

Check before an hour is up and if it's getting brown, turn the oven off and begin the next step.

When the time is up, prop open the oven door, turn off the heat and leave the cheesecake in the oven for 1 hour.

After 1 hour, remove from the oven. Cool to room temperature then chill 24 hours before serving.

Ketogenic Lemon Cheesecake Bars

Ingredients

1 (3 ounce) package sugar-free lemon gelatin

2 tablespoons lemon juice

2 (8 ounce) packages cream cheese

1 cup boiling water

Directions

Stir the boiling water into the box of jello, stirring for 2 minutes.

Add the cream cheese and lemon juice. Mix until all lumps have disappeared.

Pour into an 8" square pan and chill until set.

Cut into 8 squares.

Peanut Butter Cheesecake

Ingredients

16 ounces cream cheese, softened

1 envelope unflavored gelatin

1/4 cup cold water

1/4 cup boiling water

1/2 cup sugar free syrup, vanilla flavor

2 tablespoons natural peanut butter

2 tablespoons cocoa

1 teaspoon vanilla

1/4 cup granulated Splenda or equivalent liquid Splenda

Grated sugar free chocolate curls, optional

Directions

In a small bowl, soften the gelatin by sprinkling it over 1/4 cup cold water; let stand 1-2 minutes.

Stir in the boiling water until the gelatin is dissolved. In a medium bowl, beat the cream cheese with an electric mixer until fluffy.

Beat in the Splenda syrup, 1 tablespoon peanut butter, 1 tablespoon cocoa and vanilla. Taste, and if needed, add 1 more tablespoon each peanut butter and cocoa as well as 1/4 cup granulated Splenda.

Beat in the gelatin; pour into a 9-inch pie plate that has been sprayed with non-stick spray.

If desired, sprinkle the top of the pie with chocolate curls.

Chill 3 hours until set.

Berry Cheesecake Bites

Ingredients

Crust

½ cup Almond Flour

½ cup Coconut Flour

2 tbsp. Psyllium Husk Powder

2 tbsp. Coconut Oil

2 large Eggs

5 tbsp. Ice Cold Water

½ tsp. Pure Vanilla Extract

¼ tsp. Liquid Stevia

Filling

5 oz. Cream Cheese

1 large Egg

¼ cup Erythritol, powdered

⅓ cup Sour Cream

½ tsp. Pure Vanilla Extract

10 drops Liquid Stevia

Topping

2.5 oz Blackberries

Zest from ½ Lemon

2 tbsp. Erythritol, powdered

Directions

Mix all of the dry ingredients together for the crust, and then mix the wet ingredients slowly into the dry.

Knead the crust together and form a block. Cut the block into 4 and line the inside of a tart pan.

Cook the crust in the oven at 350F for 12-15 minutes.

Powder the erythritol in a spice grinder and use a hand mixer to mix all of the cheesecake ingredients together.

Add erythritol to the cheesecake mix and mix again. Once done, fill tart pans and cook for 25-30 minutes in the oven.

While cheesecakes are cooking, add blackberries to pan over medium-low heat. Stir berries until lightly melted.

Top the cheesecakes with the blackberry and add a scoop of whipped cream.

Keto Chocolate Mousse

Ingredients

3/4 cup whole milk ricotta cheese

1/2 cup heavy cream

1/3 cup granular Splenda or equivalent liquid Splenda

1/2 teaspoon orange extract

1/4 teaspoon vanilla

2 tablespoons cocoa

Directions

In a large bowl, beat the ricotta with all but the cocoa until it starts to thicken. Sift in the cocoa, stir to blend well, then beat briefly until very thick.

Due to some property of cocoa, it will thicken the cream in a matter of seconds, so be careful not to overbeat it.

Divide into 4 small serving dishes; chill well or freeze for about an hour before serving.

After freezing about an hour, the outside will be quite firm, but the inside will still be somewhat creamy.

Ketogenic Coconut Cream Pie

Ingredients

4 eggs

1/4 cup butter, softened

1 cup granular Splenda

1/4 teaspoon salt

1/2 teaspoon baking powder

2 cups heavy cream

1 cup coconut shavings

1 teaspoon vanilla or pineapple extract

Directions

Place all of the ingredients in a blender and blend until smooth.

Pour into a buttered 10-inch pie plate. Bake at 350F° for 45-60 minutes.

Bake less time for a more creamy pie and longer for a more firmer pie.

Key Lime Cheesecake

Ingredients

1 packet unflavored gelatin

1/2 cup lime juice, juice of 4 limes

24 ounces cream cheese, softened

2 1/2 cups granular Splenda

1 teaspoon vanilla

5 teaspoons lime zest

2 drops green food color

1 drop yellow food color

1 cup heavy cream, whipped

Whipped cream for topping

Directions

In a small pot, sprinkle the gelatin over the lime juice and let soften 5 minutes. Heat and stir over low heat to dissolve the gelatin completely.

Beat the cream cheese, Splenda and vanilla until creamy. Gradually beat in the gelatin mixture and lime zest then beat until fluffy.

Beat in the food coloring until well blended. Gently fold in the whipped cream.

Pour into a 9-inch pie plate and chill until set, about 5-6 hours. Garnish with whipped cream or Whipped Topping, if desired.

Ketogenic Almond Cookies

Ingredients

1 (8-ounce) package sugar-free chocolate-flavored snack cake mix

1 large egg, lightly beaten

2 1/2 tablespoons water

1 tablespoon almond extract

1/2 teaspoon vanilla extract

Cooking spray

50 almond slices, toasted

Directions

Preheat oven to 350°.

Combine first 5 ingredients in a bowl, stirring until blended.

Drop dough by level teaspoonfuls onto baking sheets coated with cooking spray. Press 1 almond slice into top of each cookie.

Bake at 350° for 8 minutes. Transfer cookies to wire racks, and cool completely.

Printed in Great Britain
by Amazon